I0522069

THE MODERN HIGH SCHOOL PLAYBOOK

How to Build a Successful High School
Plan to Achieve Your Goals

Brenton Mendoza Clamor

Copyright © Brenton Mendoza Clamor 2023

All rights reserved. No part of this publication may be reproduced, stored in a retrieval system, or transmitted in any form or by any means without the prior written permission of the publisher.

First Edition

ISBN: 979-8-9879060-0-2

Published by Brenton Mendoza Clamor
www.TheModernHighSchoolPlaybook.com

Acknowledgments

To my high school mentors, counselors, and all those who provided me with educational and career guidance, thank you for believing in me from the very beginning.

To my family, thank you for your unconditional love. It is the foundation of my work ethic, and it has been instrumental in helping me to achieve my goals.

And to my twin brother, who was there for me every day in high school, thank you for being my best friend. I wouldn't be where I am today without you.

Now it is time to pass your wisdom and guidance forward.

Contents

Introduction

This book is written for you if you are a student entering or currently enrolled in high school. It is meant to help you plan your high school path, starting with understanding your goals. The earlier you use this book, the more time you will have to plan and implement its practices.

Concisely written for students with busy schedules, you will learn essential tools and techniques to develop and manage your plans. You will discover how to use these skills while considering your mental and emotional well-being. I encourage you to take notes and bookmark while you read so that you can quickly refer back to what you learned.

Each high school student has their own unique goals. Some aspire to attend a prestigious university, some wish to develop practical trade skills, and others prefer to start an exciting business. Because each student comes from a different background and environment, their plans to reach their goals will vary. No matter how big your dreams or exceptional your story, this book will help you create a customized plan to achieve your goals.

Outside of this book, you are encouraged to follow @TheModernHighSchoolPlaybook on Instagram where you can continue to learn and share high school strategies with other students.

My Story

If you've made it past the first page, I assume you are a student either entering or enrolled in high school. You may be wondering why you should spend time reading this book and taking notes from someone like me. Let me explain by sharing my story.

When I started high school, I was overwhelmed and stressed. Immersed with finding my way around an unfamiliar campus and making new friends, I found it difficult to focus on one task at a time. I had so many questions. What advanced courses should I take? Should I play sports? Should I join after-school clubs? How do my classes prepare me for a successful future beyond high school? So, without a plan or priorities, I tried to do it all. I joined one too many activities, and I exhausted myself mentally and emotionally.

After my freshman year, I decided to use my time more strategically. I might not have known how to start my high school journey, but I knew how I wanted to finish it. I had one goal. I wanted to be the first generation in my family to go to college. Rest assured, this book is for any student with any goal. Going to college may have been my goal, but it is not the goal for every student.

With a goal in mind, I knew that I needed a plan. I remember asking my mom and grandma for advice, but without having experience applying to college, their best guidance was to "do my best." While I appreciated their love and support, I remember feeling alone and confused. I didn't know how to create a plan, and I didn't have a mentor who could help me.

Fortunately, I grew up with Google. I was able to research application requirements of several colleges. Following online forums and blogs, I read about the achievements of high school students who were accepted into their colleges of choice. Based on this information, I drafted my first high school plan. Without prior experience creating a plan or knowing anyone else with one, I was doubtful in my efforts. Thinking back to my family's advice, what if "my best" was not enough?

Fast forward to my high school graduation. I led a class of about five hundred students in my commencement speech as their class valedictorian. My voice wavered as I thanked my family and teachers for their support. I could recall all the stress leading up to this point and the amount of sleep I lost, worrying if my plan would help me reach my goal. Had I known about a structured process to develop a high school plan, I would have been more confident in the decisions I made. In this book, I will share this process with you so that, hopefully, you can worry less than I did.

Super-fast forward to my career, where I lead teams of engineers. My favorite part of being a leader is helping my employees develop their career plans. I help them define their ten-year long-term goals, navigate their one-year short-term goals, and manage their daily schedules. After years of leading, I've learned that planning and execution are transferrable skills. In fact, developing a career plan is very similar to developing a high school plan!

Having graduated as high school valedictorian and developing employee career plans for a living, I am writing this book to give back to high school students like you, who may share the same cloud of uncertainties about high school planning that I had while growing up. With the skills you learn from this book, I hope you will be able to confidently navigate through the unknowns of high school while trusting in your plan to reach your goals.

Define Your Goals

How many times have you been asked, "What do you want to do when you grow up?". Maybe you know what that is, and if you do, awesome! If not, don't stress. In this chapter, you will learn how to think about your goals and what to consider when defining them. Clear goals are important to your high school plan because they highlight where you need to focus your time and energy.

So, where do you start in defining your goals? Let's break down the thinking process. To begin, there are various types of goals, and it helps to categorize them into two buckets: long-term and short-term. For the context of high school, let's define "long-term" as the period after you graduate and "short-term" as the time when you are in high school.

When defining your goals, it's easiest to start with a view of the big picture by identifying your long-term goals. Next, you will define your short-term goals that help you reach your long-term goals. Then, in the following chapters, you will link your short-term goals to your high school plan. Do you see how your long-term goals, short-term goals, and plan are connected? If not, don't worry. We will be discussing these topics in more depth, and their link will become clear.

Long-Term Goals

Using this structure to think about your goals, let's start exploring your long-term goals and career options. If you have not decided on a career, think about your values. What matters to you? What makes you smile and brings you joy? What can you see yourself doing every day? Make a list of your values and what you enjoy doing. Then, see if you can find a career encompassing some of these attributes.

When thinking about your values, be aware of any factors that may bias your beliefs. For instance, say both your parents are chefs, and you are thinking of becoming one too. Before you decide, you should ask yourself if you want to be a cook because you have a passion for creating food or if it is only because you look up to your parents. In the opposite scenario, if you dislike someone, try not to rule out their profession just because you two do not get along. These are your values, your goals, your life. You do you.

As a curious teenager, it is okay if you have multiple career interests. When I was in high school, I had difficulty deciding between many professions: oceanography, medicine, aviation—you name it. However, you will need to create a plan for each career, so I recommend starting with a maximum of three choices. To help you decide, consider listing the pros and cons of each career. Then, compare the lists against each other. Also, I suggest ranking your career interests. While ranking is not important at the beginning stages of creating a plan, it will prepare you for situations when you need to prioritize. For instance, if your high school offers two electives you are interested in at the same time, you can use your rankings to help you choose one.

If you cannot identify a career that encompasses your beliefs, you will need to spend a little time researching options. Likely, there may be a career out there for you that you do not know exists. Use Google, or ask your teachers, family members, or trustworthy mentors for ideas. As the adage goes, you don't know what you don't know. Believe it or not, I didn't know anything about an engineering career in high school. I learned more about this field in college. Looking back, I wish I inquired more about job options from my high school peers and teachers so that I could have started exploring an engineering path earlier.

Remember, there are not any wrong answers to your long-term goals. If after conducting research you still cannot identify a career, make one of your long-term goals something that gives you the opportunity to find your passion. For instance, maybe you want to travel and see the world. Consider defining your long-term goal as getting accepted into a college with foreign exchange programs where you can continue exploring career options while also traveling.

Short-Term Goals

Once you understand your values and think of career options that align with them, you are ready to define your short-term goals. What do you want out of high school? How can you use your high school experience to get you where you want to go? If you are considering college, which classes will benefit your college applications?

If you want to be a doctor, you may want to aim for A's in your advanced science classes and participate in a science fair. If you want to travel, learning a different language would be an important skill. Want to start your own business? Consider making it a goal to participate in a club for entrepreneurs. If your school does not have one, consider creating your school's first business club.

Your short-term goals will be directly incorporated in your high school plan. So, when you write out your goals, make them clear and specific so that you can visualize where they fall into place in your plan. Thinking technically, some people find it helpful to remember to make their goals SMART (specific, measurable, achievable, relevant, time-bound). For instance, if you want to attend a university that typically accepts students with high test scores, develop goals to take a test prep class in your sophomore year and achieve certain scores by the end of your sophomore and junior years.

While still achievable, make sure you develop goals that push you outside of your comfort zone. Do not be afraid of these "stretch" goals. Humans are extraordinary when presented with challenges, including you. With determination and hard work, you can achieve great things! As Norman Vincent Peale famously quoted, "Shoot for the moon. Even if you miss, you'll land among the stars."

For now, brainstorm as many high school goals as you can. Later in this book, we will discuss how to set goals while accounting for your emotional and mental well-being.

Goals Summary

- Think about your values. Make sure they are your own. Align them with your long-term career goals.
- Don't worry about choosing the perfect career. Life is full of opportunities to adjust your goals.
- Be open-minded. Research long-term career options online and discuss them with your personal contacts.
- Make your short-term goals clear and specific. Do not be afraid to test your potential. You are capable of the extraordinary!

Defining Goals Reference

Your Values (e.g., Make a positive difference in the world, become financially independent from parents, be able to enjoy a work-life balance)

Long-Term Career Goals (Ranked) (e.g., A doctor who finds cures, a mechanic who fixes exotic cars)

Short-Term High School Goals (e.g., Graduate as high school valedictorian, become accepted into a four-year university with financial aid)

Download templates at www.TheModernHighSchoolPlaybook.com

Identify Your Mentors

High school is a unique chapter in everyone's life. At times, the unfamiliar situations surrounding you can feel like walking through a dark tunnel. While you are perfectly capable of making it through the tunnel alone, mentors make your travel feel less solitary and the path less dark. Think of having mentors like having a flashlight. Mentors provide guidance that illuminate new perspectives along the way.

Mentors provide a wide array of benefits, but their guidance will vary based on their background. Therefore, I recommend identifying more than one mentor as part of your high school plan.

Benefits

- Someone you can relate to so that you do not feel alone.
- Someone to clarify any myths about your chosen career.
- Someone to help you brainstorm ways to enter your career path.
- Someone to read and provide feedback on your essays for college, scholarship, and job applications.
- Someone to hold you accountable.

How to Choose a Mentor

It may be easy to identify a mentor as someone you know, such as a family member, and while these contacts may be a good place to start, oftentimes the most helpful mentors are individuals outside your immediate social circle. When choosing a mentor, keep in mind these distinct qualities.

Qualities of a Mentor

- Relatable. Your mentors should have direct or indirect experience in your post-high school interests. If you see yourself traveling in the future, is your mentor in the travel industry? If you want to be a chef, do they have their own catering business or work in a restaurant? If you want to attend an Ivy League school, are they familiar with the admissions process? Be conscious of your and your mentor's time and energy. Only spend time discussing career options with individuals who have the experience to help you.

- Trustworthy. Your interactions with mentors should feel genuine and honest. You should feel comfortable sharing your thoughts with them. Mentors are individuals you trust and always treat you with kindness and respect.

- Empowering. The best mentors leave you feeling empowered. When discussing your high school plans or goals, their constructive feedback makes you feel confident in your abilities to conquer the world. You should feel excited to see them every time you meet.

A good place to start identifying mentors is conversing with your teachers, guidance counselors, or even family members. One of the career options I explored in high school was becoming an airline pilot. Pilots piqued my interests because they looked cool in the movies, but aside from Hollywood appearances, I had no idea if I was going to enjoy sitting in the captain's seat controlling a large vehicle off the ground. I didn't know where to start in exploring this career.

So, one day after biology class, I approached my favorite high school teacher to share my situation. I asked her if she had any recommendations for where to begin. I remember her telling me to give her a week to think about it. After one week, she returned to me with good news. She knew a parent who was an airline pilot. Upon receiving the pilot's permission for me to talk with him, she passed me his phone number. I remember being so excited to call him after school that I had difficulty focusing on my classes that day. In our conversation, he asked if I would like to fly with him in a small trainer airplane to see if I enjoy flying. I couldn't believe my fortunate course of events. How many high school students get the opportunity to fly behind the yoke of an airplane? My first flight was a memory I would never forget, and it all started with asking for help from a teacher.

If you do not have a mentor identified with the qualities above, do not worry! Consider part of your plan to be finding mentors. Create short-term goals like identifying at least two mentors each year in high school.

Once you identify a mentor, ask them for their time to discuss your desired career. Check if there were any activities in high school that helped (or could have helped) them enter their profession. Do they recall any specific accomplishments? After your interview with them, take time to digest their comments and ask yourself if you are still interested in that field. Revisit your goals and update as needed based on what you learned.

After your initial conversation, consider whether it makes sense to schedule another meeting. If you are not interested in the career anymore, then obviously do not waste your time and energy. If you are still interested and found the discussion helpful, think about when it would make sense to revisit with your mentor.

The time between meetings with your mentor depends on several factors. First, it depends on when you will have new information to share. Each meeting should be productive. Providing updates and receiving feedback should take the entire meeting. Second, it depends on your mentor's schedule. If they are busy, you might annoy them with too many meetings. When in doubt, ask them when it would be best for them to meet. Third, it depends on your relationship with your mentor. If you know them personally, they may feel comfortable meeting anytime. In general, typical meeting frequencies with mentors can vary monthly, quarterly, or bi-annually. To hold yourself accountable, consider having a short-term goal to meet with at least one of your mentors on a recurring basis.

While mentors can provide huge benefits in reaching your goals, remember that their feedback is only guidance and not mandatory. Ultimately, you are in control of your career path. As an example, if one of your mentors makes drastic changes to your college application essay, you should ask yourself if it changes your story and your intent. You should never lose your own identity based on someone else's opinion.

Sometimes, someone who you thought would be a great mentor turns out to be someone who is not. Maybe your career interests no longer align or maybe their feedback no longer makes you feel excited or empowered. These situations are natural, and if they occur, limit your time and energy placed into the relationship. Politely let your mentor know that you have enough information from them that is needed. As always, be kind, and don't forget to thank your mentors.

Mentors Summary

- Identify multiple mentors who align with your long-term career goals.
- Mentors should have relatable career interests. They should be trustworthy. They should make you feel empowered.
- Consider meeting regularly with your mentors.
- Accept feedback from mentors as guidance and not as mandatory requirements.

Identifying Mentors Reference

Name of Mentor	Reason they are your mentor (e.g., Relatable, Trustworthy, Empowering)	Meeting Schedule (e.g., Monthly, Quarterly, Annually)	Additional Notes

Download templates at www.TheModernHighSchoolPlaybook.com

Develop Your Plan

So far, you should have some idea of career options that interest you and high school goals that you want to accomplish. You may have mentors picked out at this point as well. Now, we are ready for the most exciting part in creating your high school plan—visually putting it all together.

There are many templates you can use to illustrate your high school plan. I recommend starting with the basic template on the next page. You will need to transfer this template to multiple sheets of paper or one large sheet. When I mapped out my high school plan, I used legal paper (8.5" x 14") that I could find at school.

After you draft your first plan, you may have ideas on how to improve its formatting. If so, I proudly say, "GO FOR IT!". I encourage taking ownership of your plan. You may consider using different colors to prioritize and categorize information. Have fun with it.

High School Plan Template – 4 Year Semester System

Note: Update The Number of Columns As Needed to Fit Your School System

	Yr. 1 Fall	Yr. 1 Spr.	Yr. 1 Sum.	Yr. 2 Fall	Yr. 2 Spr.	Yr. 2 Sum.	Yr. 3 Fall	Yr. 3 Spr.	Yr. 3 Sum.	Yr. 4 Fall	Yr. 4 Spr.	Yr. 4 Sum.
Courses												
Extra-curriculars												
Goals												
Mentors												
Notes												

Download templates at www.TheModernHighSchoolPlaybook.com

To help fill out your plan, we will go through each of this table's elements in detail.

Timeframe Columns

Each column represents a semester in the template. By having time periods in the columns, you can compare your goals across your high school years. You will want to play around with the placement of your courses and activities. It's important to balance them over time so that you prevent one year from being highly challenging and another year extremely light. You want to push yourself towards your goals, while maintaining an overall healthy well-being.

If your school does not operate on a four-year semester system, you will need to update the number of columns. For instance, if your school operated on quarterly terms, your columns would be "Q1, Q2, Q3, Q4" for each year.

In the template, I added summer, and I recommend that you do as well. Including summer as part of your plan provides additional flexibility in accomplishing your goals, since it allows you more time to complete them. Summer can be a time when you build volunteer hours for a scholarship program or make additional income to meet a financial goal.

Courses

In addition to ensuring that you have a balanced course load throughout high school, you need to consider how you sequence your classes. Advanced courses may require satisfying prerequisites. Be sure to understand the requirements of each class when you incorporate them as part of your plan.

Also, consider how your courses can support some of your extracurricular activities. For instance, say you are interested in a career in Congress, and you want to apply for a summer political science internship. To help your chances of being accepted into the program, it may be worth taking at least one government class before you apply.

Truly, choosing classes requires careful thought. When I was exploring a career as a pilot, I needed to balance my courses and a job to pay for flight lessons. To fly for a summer, I needed to work for at least half a year. So, in the semester that I worked, I intentionally chose classes in subjects I was strong in. I saved my challenging courses for semesters when I did not work and had more time to study.

Extracurricular Activities

Extracurricular activities typically take place outside of school hours. Unlike required academic courses, they are completely voluntary. Because of the wide range of activities to choose from, you should be strategic with how you choose to spend your free time.

Most extracurricular activities should align with your career options. For instance, if you are pursuing a sports scholarship, it would make sense for one of your activities to be that sport. If you are interested in web design, check if there is an after-school club in this subject.

Also, if you need to work in high school, see if you can match your part-time job with your goals. For example, if you want to be a veterinarian, ask veterinary offices for summer internship opportunities.

If you want to participate in an extracurricular that does not directly align with your career, think about how it can help you indirectly. For instance, I enjoyed writing poetry in my free time in high school. So, I entered several online poetry scholarship competitions. I was able to use the proceeds of my winnings to support my college tuition.

Goals

In this section of the table, write your short-term high school goals for each term. It is okay for some goals to repeat (e.g., "Earn straight A's"), but check if they can be made more specific. For instance, if you have "Take PSAT/SAT" for three years in a row, consider the first year you take them to be "Obtain X Score." Then, in the second year, write "Obtain X+100 score." In the last year, aim to "Obtain X+200 Score."

Writing out your short-term goals is important because it keeps you focused and motivated. When you think back to your long-term goals, they can seem distant. Some of them may be more than ten years away. Focusing on short-term goals makes seeing the big picture easier. Like running a long-distance race, if you try to focus on the finish line five miles out, it will look discouragingly blurry. You may not even be able to see it. However, if you aim to make it to the next tree every mile, or even half mile, making it through the entire race can feel more achievable.

Additionally, writing out your goals holds you accountable. You should reference your plan several times throughout the year to constantly remind yourself of your goals. When you share your plan with your trusted mentors, they should hold you accountable as well.

Mentors

In this section, add your mentors or individuals you identify as potential mentors. Sometimes, we can get lost in the daily work of high school and feel like we are going through it by ourselves. Having your mentors identified and listed as part of your plan reminds you that you are not alone.

Notes

This section of your plan is optional to include. If you are like me, you may have thoughts and ideas that you like to write down and revisit later.

High-School Plan Summary

- Fill out the high school template in this chapter. Customize it as needed. Own your plan!
- Strategically balance your coursework and activities. Research prerequisites to properly sequence your classes.
- Implement your short-term goals in your plan and hold yourself accountable to them.

Understand Your Limits and Set Boundaries

Your potential will never be realized unless you set high goals for yourself, but it is important to recognize your limits and set boundaries so that you do not put your well-being at risk. If you are under too much stress or lack sufficient rest, you may find it difficult to perform well in your classes and activities which will compromise reaching your goals.

Understanding your limits is challenging and requires you to be introspective. Limits can be categorized into two types: internal and external. Your internal limits are your physical, mental, and emotional well-being. How much sleep does your body need to perform well? Are you someone who stresses over details? Do you have any disabilities?

External limits have to do with your surroundings and resources around you. If you stay late at school, do you have transportation to return home safely? Does your school offer SAT preparation or will you need to obtain outside tutoring? Do you have the proper academic support and guidance at school that you need to succeed?

Once you understand your limits, create goals as part of your plan to prevent you from placing your well-being at risk. For instance, if you need a mental place to escape, add reading your favorite book to your goals. If you are feeling overwhelmed, make it a goal to set aside some time during the weekend just for you, without any plans.

Everything discussed up to this point on limits and boundaries has been shared from a proactive standpoint. You want to proactively set boundary goals for yourself so that you do not exceed your limits. However, sometimes the only way to understand your limits is through experience, and you may need to think of a backup plan in case you exceed them. For instance, say you are deciding on whether you should take a semester full of advanced classes or a semester with mixed difficulty courses. In this scenario, I recommend considering a way to test your limits while preventing permanent negative consequences. Is there an opportunity for you to opt in a class for a month, and if it's too difficult, can you transfer out? Also known as "auditing" a class, you should check if this is an option with a teacher or a guidance counselor.

The more you understand your limits, the more you will understand their consequences. While consequences are never easy to face, embrace the ability to recognize them. It is easier to make decisions in developing your high school plan when you know what to expect rather than being surprised.

If you are unsure about your limitations, like the number of advanced classes you should take, I encourage you to consult with your mentors or guidance counselors. They may be able to share typical student limitations they have observed. Ultimately, however, you understand yourself better than anyone else. You can ask your parents, teachers, and counselors for guidance, but remember that it is only their opinions based on their experience.

I went to two different high schools, and the first school I attended had rules that limited the number of advanced classes I could take in my freshman year. I remember the dean and guidance counselor telling me more about what I could not do rather than what I could do. I stayed in that school for a year because of my mom's suggestion to give it a chance. Unfortunately, even after excelling in my first year, the school continued to restrict the number of advanced classes I could take. Thankfully, my mom pulled me out the second year, and I transferred high schools. In the second high school, I was unrestricted from taking any classes. Not only did I excel academically, but I learned a great deal about my potential and limitations.

Lessons learned, there will always be people who cast doubt on your abilities. It could be an individual or an institution. I hope in these times you believe in yourself and disregard them. Understand your limits and consequences, receive guidance from others, set boundaries, and confidently proceed with your plan.

Limits and Boundaries Summary

- Understand your internal and external limits. Think about your consequences in exceeding them.
- Use goals to set boundaries in your plan and prevent exceeding your limits. Never compromise your well-being.

Manage Your Plan

Once you draft the first copy of your high school plan, take a moment to pat yourself on the back. Great job! You should be proud of yourself. Having a plan is always better than not having one at all. With this said, it is important to avoid feeling too attached to your plan, and you should expect it to change many times. Throughout high school, your interests and surroundings will evolve, and consequently, so will your plan.

To manage your plan, you need to routinely check it against how you are doing. At a minimum, consider revisiting your plan at the end of every school term. Ask yourself what went well and what was challenging. Based on your experience, make changes to your courses, extracurricular activities, and your goals.

Managing Challenges

It's easy to follow a plan when you are on track, but what if you do not meet your goals at the end of a term? If not, there is no need to despair. We cannot change our past, but we can learn from it to improve our future. Reflect on why you did not reach your goals. What did you learn? What could you have done differently? Consider writing your lessons in a journal or noting them in the table of your plan discussed in the previous chapter.

Often underrated, the lessons you learn from your challenges are invaluable. They make you a better person by providing you with feedback on how to improve yourself. You may learn that you need to acquire a new skill or that you need to approach a situation with a different strategy. Also, the lessons provide you with experience in overcoming similar challenges. Next time, you will know the issues to look out for and the mistakes to avoid. Your chances of success will be greatly improved. So, while missing objectives can be disappointing, embrace the experience and learning opportunities that come with them!

Furthermore, the challenges you face and how you overcome them make influential stories. These stories have their advantages. They can help people avoid the mistakes you made. They can inspire and provide hope to individuals in similar situations. Lastly, they can prove to yourself and to others that you do not give up. Your stories are powerful, so don't forget to save them in a document. They can benefit you in job interviews and college applications.

Based on what you learn from your challenges, you will need to make updates to your high school plan. Can you move a goal that you missed to another term? Do you need to carve out time for additional study sessions? If so, do you have this time available in your schedule? You may need to be creative and move or drop activities or classes to get you back on track towards achieving your goals.

The most important part about navigating changes in your plan is to never lose confidence in yourself. Learn from your experience, stay positive, and make changes to your plan or make a back-up plan.

Multiple Career Tracks and Back-Up Plans

Sometimes we can be overly ambitious, and typically, we have a hunch when we are. If you develop a plan that seems unlikely, consider developing a back-up plan. A back-up plan is a new plan in the event the first plan does not work out.

One of my high school goals was to graduate with a two-year college degree. Incorporating a college curriculum in a high school plan is difficult because of the unpredictable availability of certain college courses throughout the year. To make sure this goal was possible, I made several back-up plans laying out various course schedules.

If you are thinking about multiple career paths, consider mapping out a plan for each profession. By mapping out each plan, you can see if there are similar courses and activities between them. Ideally, you would combine these similarities into one plan so that you have the flexibility to explore multiple career paths.

Making plans is an exercise. The more you do it, the easier it becomes. By repetitively making updates and changes, you are sorting through multiple options to converge on the best plan forward to accomplish your goals.

Capture Your Accomplishments

When you evaluate your plan at the end of each term, take the opportunity to capture your accomplishments. Be sure to save them in a journal, phone, or laptop. You should keep a running log of them to reference in the future, since it can be easy to forget what you did several years ago. This database will be helpful in times when you need to create a résumé or fill out a college or job application.

Managing Your Plan Summary

- After every high school term, reflect on your challenges and accomplishments. Update your plan based on what you learned. Document your challenges, lessons learned, and achievements.
- Be comfortable making changes to your plan, making different plans for various career paths, and creating back-up plans. The more plans you draft, the easier it is to see all your options.

Keep a Daily Schedule

At the start of this book, we looked at your long-term goals and linked them to a multi-year high school plan, but from a day-to-day basis, you may be wondering how to keep track if it all. Between studying multiple subjects and attending activities throughout the day, high school can be busy!

I recommend keeping track of your classes and activities in a daily schedule with hourly intervals. For your reference, a template is provided at the end of this chapter. Assuming your schedule is the same on a weekly basis, you should only need to map out one week. However, if your schedule differs from week-to-week, you will need to write out each week separately.

Similar to how you developed your high school plan, you should consider your limitations. Avoid cramming too many activities in one day that may lead to schedule conflicts. If you need to drive or be driven from one location to another, account for traffic. Finally, it is important to protect your overall well-being. Pencil in buffer, mental breaks, or even sleep! Just be sure to follow the schedule and hold yourself accountable.

Daily Schedule Template

Time	Monday	Tuesday	Wednesday	Thursday	Friday	Saturday	Sunday
6AM – 7AM							
7AM – 8AM							
8AM – 9AM							
9AM – 10AM							
10AM – 11AM							
11AM – 12PM							
12PM – 1PM							
1PM – 2PM							
2PM – 3PM							
3PM – 4PM							
4PM – 5PM							

Download templates at www.TheModernHighSchoolPlaybook.com

Be Curious and Research

By now, you have probably realized that creating a plan requires more time and thought than merely filling in boxes in a template. It demands strategic thinking in how you can maximize your time.

While there are multiple paths to the same goal, some routes are easier than others. After you create your high school plan, you should ask yourself, "Can I accomplish my goals in a more efficient manner?". The answer to this question requires curiosity and research.

In this chapter, we will highlight several subjects that you should consider focusing your research on.

Courses

In addition to understanding prerequisites to your classes, be aware that course availability can vary throughout the year. You may be able to find out when a course is offered if you know one of the instructors in advance. Also, you can gauge the availability of a class by looking at when they were offered in the past. Some schools may have old course handbooks that you can reference.

If you are considering college post-high school, there may be advanced high school classes that also count as college credit. However, be aware that the actual number of credits you receive is dependent on the college. For example, for the same advanced high school course completed, College A may give you four credits, College B may grant three credits, and College C may award no credits. If you are curious about the number of college credits you could receive from one of your advanced classes, you should check directly with the college.

Teachers

Every student learns differently, and every teacher has a unique instruction style. Therefore, learning is often a two-way street. This relationship can make a difference in the grade that you earn. So, if you have an opportunity to choose a course based on your instructor, take control of your learning and research the instructor. Do they engage students in discussion, or do they recite information from slides? Do they grade based on a few exams or multiple projects? How do you best learn?

There are a couple of ways that you can research your instructors. The first way is through word of mouth. Speak with your peers and reach out to someone who took the course before. The second way is to check online forums. There may be websites where students post reviews about their teachers. Be thoughtful when reading these reviews. Like posts on social media, most of them highlight extreme opinions, so you have to use your own judgement on the credibility of your sources.

Colleges and Careers

Throughout high school, your evolving interests may lead you to inspiring new career paths. As you embrace these changes, you should evaluate whether they impact your decisions about college. If a profession requires a college degree, consider researching schools that have specific programs catered to your field of interest. Some colleges may excel in mathematics, while others may be better in agricultural studies.

When choosing a college, you should check that it is accredited. You wouldn't want to study and pay for a certificate or a degree only to find that it is unrecognized by your profession. Unfortunately, there have been too many horror stories about unaccredited programs. Students who completed two years at a non-accredited college have been surprised finding out that none of their credits could transfer to another university.

When researching the best college program for your career interest, you will likely run into prestigious universities with low acceptance rates. While you should have back-up plans to attend other schools, you should never let a school's name or reputation intimidate you from applying. Truly, the first step into being admitted is self-nominating yourself. If you do not believe in yourself, it will be difficult convincing others to believe in you. So, share your story. Use what you have discovered about yourself in this book, such as your long-term goals, high school achievements, and how you have overcome your challenges and limitations.

Aside from college, if your career leads you to a trade school after high school, you should perform research on their instructors, reputation, and cost. Do the teachers have many years of on-the-job experience? If I wanted to be an automotive mechanic, I would want to learn from someone who has many years of experience working on a variety of cars. Learning from experts in their craft will help you climb a steeper learning curve than someone with less experience. Also, consider checking online reviews from graduates of the program. Is there published information on the student success rate of obtaining a job after completing the program? Where do most graduates of the program work? Finally, as with any investment, you should look into the trade program's cost. If it is expensive, at least you will know.

College Finances and Scholarships

Even though this book is not written exclusively for college-bound students, because of today's high college costs, I feel the need to provide students with insights into college finances and scholarships.

With college tuition increasing every year, it is only fair to question their affordability. However, a school's cost should be carefully weighed against its graduate's statistics and financial aid. Research if there is data on the college's average amount of student debt after graduation. Check if the school has a proven track record sending graduates into the workforce with high salaries.

Also, you should not rule out any college until you receive their financial aid package. For a general idea on the amount, you may be able to find their endowment fund published online. Schools with high endowment funds typically have the means to provide large financial aid packages.

Coming from a financially challenged background, I thought going to an Ivy League school would be impossible. Even if I was accepted, I was certain that I wouldn't be able to afford tuition. My application was submitted purely out of personal curiosity to see if I could get in. I didn't even tell my parents that I applied because I didn't want to engage in a financial discussion that I knew they could not support.

Surprisingly, I received a letter of acceptance followed by a generous financial aid package. With this package, the final cost of attendance was similar to the cost of a local public university.

In addition to financial aid, one of the best ways to pay for college is through scholarships. While some scholarship programs apply to multiple schools, be aware that some colleges offer additional scholarship programs specific to them. So, as soon as you identify a potential college you are interested in attending, you should check their admission's website for any internal scholarships. Furthermore, make sure to understand the requirements of each scholarship. You may need a certain number of credits, GPA, or test score to be considered. Once you know these requirements, implement them as goals in your high school plan.

By searching online, you may be surprised by the number of scholarships available. Most of these scholarships require essays. To kill two birds with one stone, check if you can use the same essays for your scholarship and college applications.

When thinking about college costs, there are many ways to bring them down. For instance, you may be able to find ways to save on room and board by looking at local housing alternatives. For books, there are multiple online venues that sell them used.

If you want to earn a four-year university degree, but not directly after high school, consider completing your first couple of years at a community college and transferring to a university later. However, recognize there are pros and cons to this scenario. While you will be saving money, you will miss out on making valuable on-campus connections with your peers and professors.

Typically, college is worth the investment, but factoring in costs, some universities may be better options than others. If you are considering taking out a large student loan to attend a private college for a low salary career, it may be worth investigating more affordable colleges. When in doubt, consider discussing college options with your mentor.

For many of you, taking out a student loan may be the first debt you incur. While it is easy to think optimistically that you will pay it all back, you should understand that student debt has long-term consequences, and it can delay your future investments like a down payment for a home.

Constructive Comparisons

Wherever you want to go after high school, it helps to compare your plans and goals with others who have similar paths. For example, if you want to go to business school, you should understand a typical applicant's GPA, extracurricular activities, or standardized test scores. If you want to be a professional sports player, you should research what others have done to improve their chances of being scouted. By comparing your plans with others and being open minded, you can learn different approaches and gain new ideas to reach your goals. Each plan you look at is like adding a new tool to your toolbox, and the more versatile your toolbox, the more creative you can be with developing your plan.

There are several ways you can compare your plans. Searching online, you can find many success stories of high school students achieving their goals. Specific to college, a university may publish average statistics of their applicants. In addition to internet research, if you have a mentor or someone you look up to with similar career passions, you can ask them to walk you through their high school plan and achievements. Also, you can reach out to a guidance counselor who may be able to use their experiences in working with other students.

If done constructively, comparing your plans with your peers is a great way to gain ideas in how to improve your plans. However, be aware that other students may not be as prepared as you to share their plans. Some students may feel competitive, shy, insecure, or intimidated. Therefore, it is important to be respectful when discussing your career plans and goals with others.

At times, comparing your plans with others may reduce your self-esteem. It is easy to look at someone's achievements and feel less significant. After all, the grass is always greener on the other side. In times like these, remind yourself that everyone's background and paths are different. With your unique story, you have the ability to achieve your career goals, just like any other student. If you ever feel overwhelmed by negative thoughts, consider taking a break from comparing your plan to others. Worrying and thinking negatively is neither mentally healthy nor productive for achieving your goals.

Research Summary

- Always be curious about your options in high school. Research courses and teachers to make informed decisions about your class schedule.
- If you have the option, choose a teacher with an instruction style that matches how you learn.
- Investigate the accreditation status of colleges and their average financial aid/scholarships granted to students.
- Before applying to trade school programs, examine their cost and reputation in supporting graduates find a job.

Celebrate Milestones

C elebrate when you complete the first draft of your high school plan. Celebrate every milestone. Celebrate the small wins. Celebrate you. Sometimes when you reach for a long-term goal, it is easy to forget the short-term goals along the way, but it is so important not to forget them!

Celebrating your wins throughout your plan is as important as a refreshment station is to a marathon runner. If you observe a marathon race, you will notice there are several checkpoints with tables of water, electrolyte drinks, and energy snacks that runners can pick up to refuel. Without these refreshments, running for hours would be too physically taxing. So, when tackling your long-term goals, make sure to prepare for the marathon, celebrate along the way, and refresh your health.

Everyone recognizes themselves differently. There is no wrong way to do it. Enjoy a peaceful walk, maybe even put on some music. Enjoy reading your favorite novel or watching a movie with a friend. As long as you dedicate time to yourself to do something that you enjoy, you are celebrating the right way.

Celebrating is not only a time to treat yourself, but also a time to reflect on your journey thus far. What did you learn? How did you grow? When you achieve a goal, there is always some kind of personal growth. Whether it was committing to a deadline or putting in extra hours to study, make sure to give yourself the recognition that you deserve.

As a word of caution, while it may be nice to receive recognition from others, try not to expect it. If you expect others to celebrate each of your wins, you will be setting yourself up for disappointment. The truth is that nobody knows the amount of work it takes for you to accomplish your goals. They are simply not you. So, do yourself a favor and be the first person to pat yourself on the back, guaranteeing that your hard work does not go unnoticed.

By recognizing your own achievements, you will improve your understanding of the hard work behind other people's achievements. You will be able to empathize with them, and consequently, you will find it easier to build a relationship with them, hopefully even a friendship. Having a network of hard-working friends is very powerful. Together, you can help each other accomplish your goals in ways like forming a study group or proofreading each other's college application essays.

When I was in high school, I was guilty of keeping my head down and grinding day and night with little to no breaks. I was so focused on my long-term goal that I lost sight of my small wins along the way. Without giving myself recognition, I remember breaking down at night from stress and fatigue. I became burnt out. Looking back, I could have minimized the emotional distress I felt in high school if I gave myself permission to enjoy my achievements in the present.

Celebrating Milestones Summary

- Be kind to yourself and celebrate each win, no matter how big or small.
- Celebration can take the form of any recognition, as long as you dedicate the time to give yourself the credit that you deserve.

Learn Together

Everyone walks a unique path in high school, and it is natural for students to feel lonely in facing their challenges. However, the reality is quite the opposite. Everyone is in the same boat, learning and improving themselves while navigating towards a successful future beyond high school.

Through transparency, you can help each other out. I encourage you to share your high school plans. The more plans you look at, the more ideas you will have to streamline them. Share your lessons learned and learn from each other. Support others and they will support you.

To start the conversation, you can follow the Instagram account below and share goals, plans, and strategies with other students. In collaborating with each other, you will find that no matter where you are in your high school journey, you are not alone. If you prefer to provide information anonymously, you can send a direct message to the Instagram account below or to the e-mail address found in the Contact section of the book's website.

Instagram: @TheModernHighSchoolPlaybook

Website: www.TheModernHighSchoolPlaybook.com

Final Notes

Having a high school plan shows you the path to achieve your goals. With a plan, hard work, and perseverance, your potential is limitless.

Remember, your plan will change. Change is natural and is part of life. Trust the process outlined in this book, manage your progress, and evolve your plan as needed. Learn from other students and pay it forward by sharing your lessons learned.

I believe in you. You got this! Enjoy high school, and I wish you success wherever your path leads you.

About the Author

In high school, I juggled academics, honors societies, and varsity athletics while taking college courses, flying airplanes, working part time at a sandwich shop, and volunteering at libraries and a petting zoo. I graduated as a high school valedictorian with a two-year college degree. Raised with limited financial means, I was the first person in my family to go to college.

Now, it is my turn to pay it forward, and this book is written to help high school students who might be unsure where to begin in navigating their high school experience and how to prepare for what lies beyond it. While I am no genius, I am someone with a high work ethic and skilled at making plans. Having a plan and visually mapping my high school courses and activities, I was able to find a path to accomplish my goals.

As a mid-career leader in today's corporate world, I continue mentoring others in developing career plans that help them reach their highest potential.

www.ingramcontent.com/pod-product-compliance
Lightning Source LLC
Chambersburg PA
CBHW070451130626
46553CB00006B/2355